OPEN PRAIRIES

OPEN PRAIRIES

Poems of Reflection on a Life in Texas

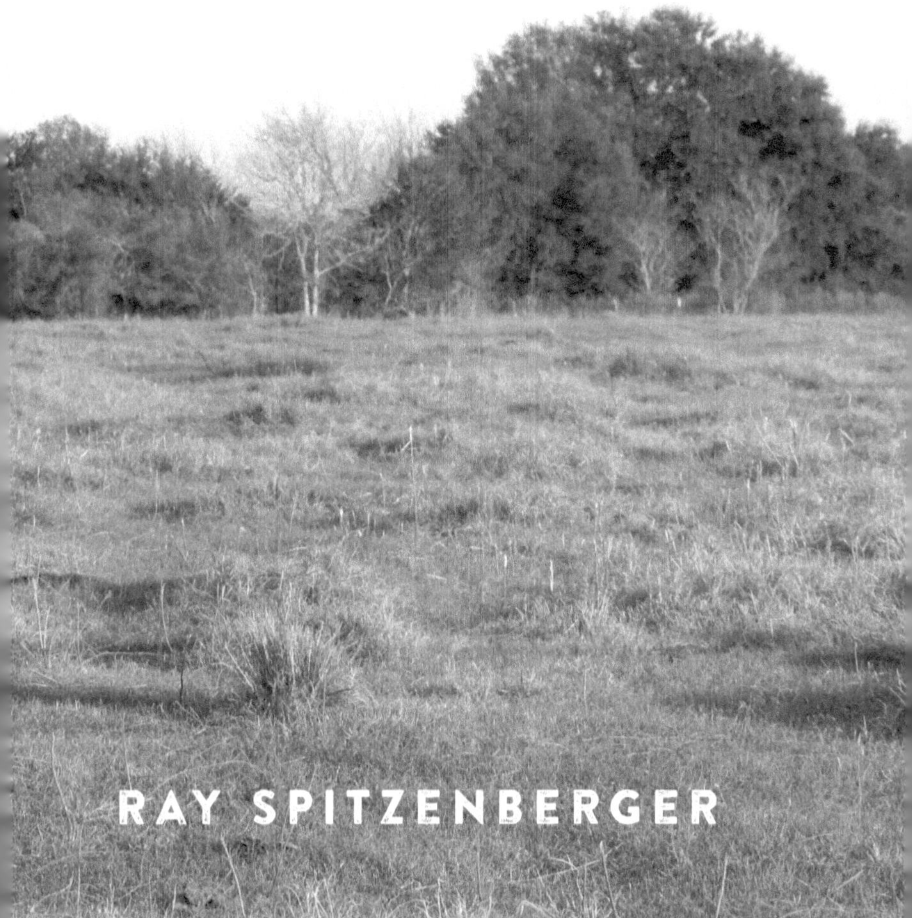

Inquiries about this book should be addressed to: Ray Spitzenberger; PO Box 575; East Bernard, Texas; or rspastorpal405@gmail.com.

Printed by Kindle Direct Publishing

Photography by Lauren Stolle
Book design by Rae Ann Spitzenberger

ISBN 979-8-6486-8621-2

In memory of my father,
Max Christian Spitzenberger,
not because he was a poet, or even that
he liked poetry, but because his humble,
gentle, kind, and caring nature
was itself a beautiful poem.

CONTENTS

INTRODUCTION IX

Memories
1

Reflections
29

Prairie Life
53

Chuckles
79

ACKNOWLEDGMENTS 98

Introduction

IT'S MUSIC TO MY EARS! THAT'S THE WAY I'VE ALWAYS thought of poetry. Not that I'm a musician, because I'm not, but I am a writer, and I especially like writing poetry, because it is the one way that I am able to "make music" with words.

When I finished my lighthearted, non-fiction prose book, *It Must Be the Noodles*, and it received a better-than-expected response from readers, I intended to write a sort of sequel to *Noodles*, but I found that the inner writer in me could not proceed with the project, even after preparing a careful outline and summaries of planned chapters. All I wanted to do was write poetry, and an inner voice kept urging me to prepare and publish a book of my poems.

Being a practical-minded German-Wend, I kept arguing with that unrelenting voice within that nobody reads poetry anymore and nobody buys books of poetry, so I need to write what readers want. Eventually, however, after rereading many of my poems, both published and unpublished, I decided that the kind of poems I write would appeal to my readers who enjoyed *It Must Be the Noodles* so much. I write poems about my life, and about life in general, as I perceive it; and so they are earthy poems, even, one could say, "rural" poems. Why wouldn't "salt of the earth" readers identify with such poems and enjoy reading them? After all, the only difference between my prose and my poetry is the music.

Besides, I believe that poetry should be written for everyone, not just for the literati, not just for English teachers, not just for subscribers of literary magazines, but for everyone. After all, as those of us former English teachers know, the first English poems were written in beer halls by rough and tough soldiers, *Beowulf* a case in point.

Those early Old English poems were meant to be sung or chanted in the beer halls to the accompaniment of usually a single musical instrument. They had rhythm, alliteration and picture language. After centuries, English poetry evolved, changed, and went in many directions, but the element of music never disappeared. The examples that some folks might cite, where music has disappeared, are not poems in my opinion—call them "poetic prose" if you want, but not "poetry."

That does not mean I write mostly rhyming poetry. I don't! I write an occasional poem with end-rhyme, but most of the time I write free verse, or I use non-rhyming

Japanese verse forms like the Haiku and the Tanka, or I use internal rhyme (I have always liked rhyming within a line rather than at the end of each line). The idea that rhyming, alliteration, and foot and meter are necessary to produce music is not valid in my opinion. I used to love to write poems in perfect iambic pentameter, or even dazzle the reader with some dactylic trimester, but those artificial rhythms are not as musical as the natural rhythms of the beautifully awesome English language itself. And, besides, when using these devices, the poet allows the end-rhyme to lead him to say what he really did not intend to say, or the trochaic tetrameter causes him to be wordy rather than musical.

In recent years, I have published in numerous poetry journals and literary magazines, both online-only and print publications, and while they still will include traditional rhyming poems, most of the poems are free verse, even experimental verse, and Americanized Japanese forms. "Americanized" is good, in that the Japanese language and the English language are so different that something meaningful is lost if you maintain the Japanese syllable count, such as 5-7-5 for the Haiku. For the Haiku, I am more likely to use a general short-long-short form rather than a definite syllable count, letting the English language itself develop the rhythm in its natural cadence.

That's enough "literary" talk, but I thought it was necessary to set the stage for the kind of poetry I write. John

Ciardi once said at a writers' workshop I attended at Ole Miss that a poem must suggest more than it explicitly states. I believe, for the most part, that's a true statement, and I hope my poems have that kind of depth, and, at the same time contain the music I believe all poems should have. I write about the simple things in life—prairie life, gardening, a yard full of birds, kittens playing, the laughter of grandchildren, Christmas lights, growing old, etc. Although I taught English literature in college for many years, I make no pretensions of being part of the literati. I live in East Bernard, Texas, often jokingly called "East Barnyard," and I love my simple, stress-free, prairie life— the reason I call this book *Open Prairies*.

Memories

FOR ME, THE NUMBER ONE INSPIRATIONAL SOURCE FOR creating poems is memory, because memory itself has a way of turning something plain and drab into something of extraordinary beauty. Poets tend to develop "creative memories," which generate poems already synthesized from various stored remembrances. Time allows memories to "ripen," perhaps sometimes too much, but always emotional, even sentimental. There are those who write poems that teach and preach, with or without emotion, but that's not what I do. For me, emotion and sentimentality are a good thing, and I don't apologize for the sentimentality in my poems.

Emotions are the refiner's fire. Difficulties, loss, struggle, suffering, loneliness, joy, happiness, awe, love, etc., refine the inner spirit and help resurrect memories in a positive way. I want a poem not only to "sing," but also to "feel."

Memory produces both history and poetry, and sometimes they are the same. I love history, but it is my belief that history books would be more fun to read if they were written as poetry rather than in prose. Just imagine the poetic possibilities in a poem about Napoleon's invasion of Russia in the winter and his subsequent defeat. Actually, I did write such a poem.

THIS EASEFUL HOUR
MADE HALCYON

the time,
childhood
the church,
rural,
the moon,
large,
lighting up the outside
the gasoline lanterns,
pumped,
lighting up the inside
the wheezing sounds
of the old pump organ
open vespers with plainsong
mama, the organist,
pumping and playing,
her fingers and feet
temporarily
freed of rheumatism
by the music
sifting through her mind and heart

   RAY SPITZENBERGER

the kindly old pastor,
in cassock and surplice,
slow-moving and serene,
lights the candles himself
this easeful hour
made halcyon
by homily, hymns and prayers
in the midst of bellicose news
from the blood-stained trenches
of a world at war

Originally published in Reflections from the Texas Cradle,
November 2018 (My childhood memory of World War II)

GRANDPA'S OLD PLOW.

grandpa's old plow
stands proudly in my yard
as a monument
to crops planted
and crops harvested
the work horses who pulled it
were no Lipizzaners
white stallions trotting on the spot
nor were they Budweiser Clydesdales
no
they were strong, long-suffering mares
pulling plows and cultivators
      endlessly
under the blistering Texas sun
their rewards were the shade of the barn
and the well-filled feed trough
and grandpa's love
yet like Lipizzaners and Clydesdales
they were proud
proud to be
plowers
pullers
endurers
doers

proud to serve the old man
who worked as hard as they
man and horses now gone
only the plow stands

THE WASH KETTLE

the old wash kettle in my backyard
hides its history well
birds sit on its rim
and lazily take sips of its cool water
dipping beaks in between floating water poppies
tall, aquatic grasses line the inside
and offer shade and places to hide
this giant old iron pot
sits in the middle of floral elegance
as if to hide its boorish past
every Monday of its bygone life
it was used to boil water on wash day
in winter, during hog-killing time
when soap supplies ran low
it became a bubbling vat of lard and lye
to produce soap strong enough
to peel your skin off
it can't tell its history, and I won't
at least not to the granddaughters
who take pictures in front of it
in their exquisite, new Easter dresses

THE JOY AND LAUGHTER
STILL LIVE IN MY HEART

At the end of a back road

In Texas,

My daddy owned a saloon,

Where his regulars washed down

His peppery chili with mugs

Of cold beer.

He always kept a few bottles

Of red soda water

Just for us,

Often my brother and I would wander off

From home,

Down the rutted street

And slip in the back door of the saloon.

Daddy always laughed

When he saw us peep

Around the corner

Of the long, massive bar,

Running into his arms,

Knocking over the brass spittoon.

The joy and laughter still live in my heart!

EMACIATED

the old church stands alone
on the sun-seared prairie
along Texas Highway 21
the emaciated old pastor,
still wearing his cassock,
shuffles across the churchyard
to the parsonage
way past lunch time,
he hasn't eaten . . .
and won't
food, while necessary,
has no allure
time, while constant,
has no importance
occasional cars and trucks hurtle by
as though trying to fast-forward themselves
past the desolate prairie,
never noticing the old church
nor the old man in the black skirt
food and time have much
meaning for them,
or so they think . . .

     RAY SPITZENBERGER

should he water the lawn
or take a nap?
his home phone ringing
tells him neither
a parishioner needs him
he smiles warmly
and tenderly looks out at the emaciated prairie

Originally published in Reflections from the Texas Cradle,
November 2018

HOW MANY TIMES?

As a child,
How many times
Didn't I give you socks for
      Father's Day?
And how many times
Didn't you react
As though I had given you
      a Pot of Gold?
It's funny how I never thought
Of giving anything else,
Believing that nothing else
Would bring the huge warm smile
That spread across your face
And turned on the lights
      in your eyes.
I knew you knew I loved you.

GINGERBREAD MEN LIVED
AT GRANDMA'S HOUSE

At Christmas,
Gingerbread men lived at Grandma's house.
They were forged in her cast iron oven
And carefully tucked into the stone crock
                by the stove,
Baker's dozens upon baker's dozens of them,
Each one just like the other.
Raisin eyes and cherry mouths,
They seemed to say, "Merry Christmas"
                to us as we came in
                to build a house for them.
O what Christmas memories the smell of gingerbread
                has for us!

THIS LAND

this land
with its deep woods and boyhood trails
this land
which had belonged to my parents
and to my grandparents before that
this land
with its large cedar brake
pin oak trees and native pecans
Johnson grass and cactuses
Mustang grape vines and thick wild blackberry brambles
which want to grab hold of you and not let you go
this land
with its weathered barn and chicken houses
now empty and ghostlike
and its old house, built from planks
from the even older farmhouse
all of it, all of it together
will soon be sold
selling this land, these buildings, this house
is like selling my childhood and my family history
I recoil at the thought of peddling off this my heritage
to a stranger
when it becomes his property

   RAY SPITZENBERGER

he will grow his children on it
and he will live out his family history on it
this land
which was my land

THE QUILT REMAINS

the quilt remains
the quilter, no more
a life measured
in tiny stitches
and pricked fingers

INDEPENDENCE, TEXAS

We sat among the buffalo clover at Old Baylor,
One and a half new Baylor girls and I,
Our hair blowing in the wind.
The tired old trees leaned against the sky,
Their Spanish beards blowing in the wind,
Behind the tall pillars in a dilapidated hall
        cactuses were growing in the wind.
Silently, we ate our lunch in silence,
Listening to the wind-voices from the hall
Sing their alma maters to us.
We arose from among the buffalo clover,
One and a half new Baylor girls and I,
And passed between the pillars,
Through the arch,
Past the cactuses,
Down the hill,
Our hair blowing in the wind.
We left Old Baylor,
One and a half new Baylor girls and I,
Wind voices following us all the way home.

Originally published in Try Magazine, *1977*

THE MAGIC ROAD

a strip of enchantment
from gate to farmhouse
about a half mile long
an oft traveled short lane
strangely colored rocks lying roadside
in drifts spilled into the ditch
like driftwood washed into the dunes
the road was often changed overnight
by the heavy, drenching rains
from hard ruts to mud and slush
followed by the fierce Texas sun
baking the mud and rocks together
into huge lumps of adobe
wildflowers often grew and bloomed
between the ruts
scissor-tailed flycatchers sat
on barbed-wire fences
showing off their long tails
it's a spell-binding road
that spills out of my dreams
of childhood days of innocence
spent in indolence
and somnolence
at my grandfather's farm

it did not prepare me
for the demanding reality
of the roads of experience
O how I wish
I could follow
that magic road
back into my childhood

THE LITTLE MUSIC BOX

When I bought the little music box
That played "Lara's Theme" from *Dr. Zhivago,*
We had just met,
But had not dated,
Had not held hands, or kissed.
In fact, we were almost strangers,
Except that your aunt,
With whom I spent
Many stuffy Sunday evenings,
Talked and talked and talked about you,
Until I wanted to shout, "Enough already!"
You, who lived far away,
Were a phantasm created in
Your old spinster aunt's mind,
Something unreachable, untouchable,
An illusion, a delusion,
This phantasm who sang opera off Broadway
      in New York,
Recordings of whose arias I was forced to listen to
By your old aunt
Who said she knew why I bought
      the music box
That played "Lara's Theme" from
      Dr. Zhivago.
You came and threw a monkey wrench
Into the life of a stuck-in-a-rut,

Not-too-young-anymore, bachelor.
It all started with your crawling on the floor
And barking like a dog
When I met you
At your aunt's house.
Why couldn't you have been like her,
Old and monotonous and annoying,
So that I could have slammed the front door
And walked away for good!
She knew that I had fallen in love
With you,
The very moment I saw you
Crawling on the floor
And barking like a dog,
And that I bought the little music box
Which played "Lara's Theme" from
          Dr. Zhivago,
And which I played
Over and over and over again,
Until I finally gave it to you.
It was then
That the most splendid music on earth
          began
And has never
          stopped.

GIRL IN TUB # 1

aquatic nymph
sporting in bathtub aquarium
of aquatic toys
adding your own aqua vitae
in a suboceanic stream
of yellow

Originally published in Try Magazine, *1977*

WAGON UNDER TREE: A TANKA

wagon under tree
faded red with muddy sides
now empty, wheel-less
long ago, two Texas tots
harnessed their daddy for rides

Originally published in Atlas Poetica 32,
A Journal of World Tanka, *2018*

MY MEG WAS A DANCER

my Meg was a dancer
she danced and danced and danced
in aerial artistry
she flew
she floated
she flagrantly flouted gravity
swirling
on her toes
she seemed to be spinning
above the footlights
kindling audible gulps
from the audience
and winning their hearts
as she danced and danced and danced
wondering why
what she did mattered

  RAY SPITZENBERGER

MY RAE-RAE WAS A THINKER

Even as a child,
My Rae-Rae was a thinker.
Her thoughts were longer
Than "the long, long thoughts of youth."
My Rae-Rae was a thinker.
She wanted to know
"If kittens knew they were kittens."
At age three, she drew a cartoon balloon
With a whale inside.
"What is that?" I asked.
"Aunt Sybil dreaming about a whale,"
         she replied.
My Rae-Rae was a thinker.
She loved Mr. Rogers,
Who told his young viewers one day
That "soporific" meant "tending to cause
         sleepiness."
"Can you make a sentence with 'soporific'?
         he asked.
"Yes," she replied.
To the smiling face on the screen,
"I have a very soporific pastor."
My Rae-Rae was a thinker.

TANKA ABOUT THE DEATH OF A LOVED ONE

sun-splashed summer day
so like other summer days
home after funeral
house in darkness with blinds shut
wanting blinds open again

Originally published in Poetry Quarterly, Winter 2017

HAIKU FOR EPIPHANY

the silent deaf boy
gently touched the organ's pipes
and heard God's voice

Originally published in 50 Haikus, Issue #13, *March 2017*

COFFEE TIME

five old men
drank coffee
at Macdonald s
every day
at exactly the same time
the two of us sat
down the aisle
across from them
once a week
weeks months years
diminished their number
until there were three
the two of us continued
our weekly coffee and chat
down the aisle
across from them
until
there was only one of us

JAZZ

jazz
Uptown
jazz
in the Lou
jazz
in the Big Easy
jazz
in Bayou City
Monk and Mingus and Basie
Roach and Tatum and Goodman
Ellington and Armstrong and Blakey
jazz
beyond the sax
jazz
beyond the keyboard
jazz
words and rhymes and syntax
vowels and consonants and spaces
found
on the leaves of literary journals
penned by Dave Oliphant
who is alive and well and somewhere in Chile

Reflections

"REFLECTION" TO A PHYSICIST IS THE CHANGE IN DIRECTION of a wavefront, such as in the reflection of light or the reflection of sound. Reflection of light occurs, for example, when light bounces off a mirror, but in "refraction" of light, the light bends as it goes through water, for example. With sound, "reflection" can cause "echoes," as well as "sound," a phenomenon that allows dolphins to navigate.

"Reflection," in literature is different. In physics, it is a physical process; but, in literature, a mental one, though the physical process could serve as a metaphor of the mental. Reflection is a mental process wherein concepts, insights, opinions, etc., are produced by contemplation.

Through the magic of poetry, a writer can release his inner thoughts in a flowing manner that prose doesn't allow. The poet, especially writing about open prairies, woodlands, and wildlife, needs to be impressionistic and suggestive, not scientifically accurate. Reflections are images that flow out of peak moments of thought and reflecting back upon. You can see the influence of William Wordsworth and other British Romantic poets in such thinking.

Japanese poetry uses an excellent three-line poetry form called "Senryu" (also known as "Human Haiku") which reflects upon human nature, often with irony and satire, in very few words. I often express my reflections in Senryu, because of the challenge it offers.

HOPE

Is hope a whisper
Or is it a shout?
Or is it
    sotto voce —
You sorta do
And you sorta don't?
That makes hope merely
    wishful thinking.
God says faith is being sure
Of what we hope for,
And hope is an anchor
    for the soul.
An anchor is not silent, —
It makes an explosive splash
Upon entering the sea,
And a loud clank
When it lands in rock!
Faith, hope, and love are
The three virtues of Grace.
The greatest is love,
But the anchor is hope.

LIKE A BAZOOKA

life gives
instead of prizes
surprises
like a bazooka
blowing you apart
maybe that's why
internet was conceived
searching for rilke reike nikes
and maybe even like keys
you can live in facebook
but when you emerge
the bazookas are still there
old and thuddy
they used to kill tanks
now covered with cobwebs
in museums
seek faith
it knows how to stop
bazookas

Originally published in Red River Review, *November 11, 2017*

OLD ADAGE

"we see things as <u>we</u> are
not as <u>they</u> are"
is probably
the oldest adage
in the world
understood more fully
by those with
dental implants and
knee replacements
hardly ever by
young people with parental-help requirements
one day the truth will find them
and splatter their preconceptions
like a Midwestern tornado
ripping through
      America's heartland

SONGS OF THE MOON

Sam Cooke sang about a Blue Moon,
Neil Young sang about a Pink Moon,
Sunset Rubdown sang about Silver Moons,
Deftones sang about a Black Moon,
Erykah Badu sang about an orange moon,
and
"When My Moon Turns to Gold Again"
was Elvis Presley's song.
But none sang about
"The Super Blood Wolf Moon"
hanging over the earth
Sunday night,
as I stood in my yard in eerie light,
hearing the phantom prairie wolves howling and howling,
scowling my face to look upward at the Moon's face
until dizzy, I swayed on my walking cane,
my eyes stalking the blood red moon till it
went dark
an awesome omen,
a foreboding bodement,
of the fear some of us feel
about our politically divided country
as though impending chaos
has cast its shadow on the land

STARRY NIGHTS

the stars
in Van Gogh's *Starry Night*
roll through the sky
like celestial bowling balls
a jolting contrast to
Starry Night Over the Rhone
painted nearly a year earlier
wherein the stars
simply light up the sky
like giant fireflies
while the long light reflections
of the lighted homes
cast light stripes
across the river
the river lights outshine the star lights
as a teenager
Vincent was taught
by his mother
that God's promise is
"to make light out of darkness
and out of problems,
good things"

why is a September sky
different
from a sky in June?
or is it the difference between
an Arles' sky and
a Saint-Remy sky?
the endless river divides at Arles
how can even the infinite sky
compete with the great Rhone?
whether in night sky
or in night river
the light shines through darkness
and out of problems come good things

PETER HURD IS ALIVE AND WELL

Peter Hurd is alive and well
in egg tempera in a museum in Roswell,
the chenille-covered mountains
circling him like a wagon train.
Peter Hurd is alive and well
in egg tempera in a museum in Roswell . . .

Originally published in The East Bernard Tribune, *July 29, 1992*

     RAY SPITZENBERGER

FOUR HAIKU TO REFLECT UPON

raking leaves in piles
burst of wind blows them away
so, too, thoughts scattered

old, skeleton trees
awake and yearn to bud out
late blizzard blows in

day lilies charm us
sunflowers captivate us
too soon summer ends

birdbath basin held
high by four stony sea creatures
water for live fowl

LET THERE BE LIGHT

to the right you are
pulled into the darkness
to the left
you are pulled into the light
the terrace of Van Gogh's café
glows with other worldly luminosity
so enticing, so seductive
so like a bright porch light
attracting moths and dragonflies
the dragonfly not nocturnal
the light luring him to his death
"The night is more alive
and more richly colored
than the day," Vincent wrote
it's hard to notice the stars
some as big as table tops or plates
the terrace pulls you away
from their lambency
the one tree disappears into the night
it's part of the darkness
like in Vincent's other night paintings

dragonflies run from the darkness
but they run to the wrong light
lonely men
like dragonflies
seek the wrong light
there are bright lights
in the brothels
and in the cafes
is it the hearthside fire
with woman and baby?
or is it beyond the galaxies
in the swirls of starfire?
Van Gogh sought and sought

FLYING SOUTH

when geese fly South
they know what they're doing
they know where they're going
they are structured
they fly a V-formation
led by a steadfast leader
humans stopped flying South
some time ago
when structure ends
life becomes a labyrinth
for the lost
no doubt that's why
growing up for me
was a long pilgrimage
away from mom and dad
only problem was
even though it was going away
from one thing
it was going toward something else
in those days
we thought we knew
what something else was
or where it was

like geese flying South
but
South either got redefined
or disappeared
we didn't have a gps
to guide us
but it would've been useless
in the maze
of cul-de-sacs
spawned by the nihilism
of war, Beats, and hopelessness
one day I found
a pilgrim's road again
and it led me
back
to the faith
that had been
with me
in the beginning

IS WHAT THERE IS ALL THERE IS?

which life-hurt hurts the most?
without a doubt
loss
no job, no friends
no place to go
no place to be
no hope for another set of tomorrows
no returning
only yearning
retreating
deleting
all that was
is what there is
all there is?
my faith says
there is more
much more
believe it!

LIFE'S ROADS

Whether through some bumpy sections,
Or around a mountainous curve,
Life's roads may cause you to swerve
In unexpected directions.
Have courage and strength in those times of strife
By knowing God and your friends stand with you,
Remaining steadfast and true,
Girding you to find kinder roads of life
In those unexpected directions.

TWO SENRYU ABOUT LIFE

If life's a circus
And God ringmaster with whip,
We go in circles.

No, life is more like
A donkey basketball game,
Yet God loves us all.

A FATHER'S LOVE

A father's love is
        like a smooth stone
        in a swift stream,
        giving of itself.
A father's love is
        like an oak tree,
        it never stops growing.
A father's love is
        like a piece of leather,
        tough and resilient.
A father's love is
        like a gust of music
        that restores and uplifts.
A father's love is
        like the sky,
        it is unlimited.
Yes, a father's love embraces so much!

 RAY SPITZENBERGER

ONLY A FATHER CAN SEE

When you're older,
And you've become a father yourself,
You remember the father
Who raised you
And you exactly understand
Why he exulted
In all that you did
And in all that you became.
Only a father can see
The conquering spirit in your eyes,
The need to make the world
A better place to live.
He has passed it on,
These heart-thoughts,
For which you daily give thanks.

MY BRIDE: SWIRLS OF LIGHT

My bride of 44 years,
You light up my universe!
Like a Van Gogh painting,
Swirls of light upon swirls of light,
Your lights bring support, comfort, and constancy
When my world darkly dims.
To say I value our life together
Is the understatement of understatements.
But then, through our great bond,
I know you know
How I feel . . .
But I'll say it again,
You light up my universe!

HAIKU ABOUT PEGGY

like bright Christmas lights
her radiant, sparkling eyes
shine heart's love inside

HAIKU ABOUT MEG

daughter, mom, teacher,
bright eyes sparkle like her mom's
reflect joyful heart

HAIKU ABOUT RAE ANN

eyes, cerulean blue
hair, fine, nephilian silk
eyes reflect keen mind

 RAY SPITZENBERGER

STARSHINE IN THREE HAIKU

each night
in the milky way
starshine

little lights
like angels with candles
dappled in light

one star
falls . . . or flies away
grab it

Prairie Life

GROWING UP IN THE RURAL TOWN OF DIME BOX, TEXAS, I enjoyed racing my bicycle down the many low hills, though it was not much fun pedaling up those hills. My family didn't own any riding horses, so I missed out on wild rides, galloping horseback across the meadows. Often walking in the sunlit meadows, I did enjoy observing the thick assortment of tall Texas grasses and wildflowers swaying in the wind like skinny, drunken prairie alligators, also known as walking stick insects.

In later years, when I moved to the Mid-Gulf Coast, I was captivated by the endless open prairies, whose tall grasses hid splendid wildlife, such as prairie chickens, egrets, wild geese, small lizards, and other prairie creatures. I loved the hills, and still do, but they didn't seem to offer the exhilarating freedom of the endless prairies.

Because of my love of rural life, I have lived in cities for only a very short length of time, feeling trapped and miserable there. To be sure, my poems have mostly been about the open prairies, small rural towns, rolling hills, prairie creatures, and other connections to nature, as seen through my Christian faith. Those are the things that bring music to my poems.

REFINED INTO THE GOLDEN YEARS?

I live where the warm prairie winds
blow across the Gulf plains,
where it's fiercely hot
during the day,
whether it rains or whether it does not,
and just as hot
at night
as I maneuver through my declining years,
life for me is rustic, peaceful, and pleasant
our home is safe and simple and comfortable
and typically rural American
our food is plain and nutritious and plebian
and overly plentiful
did the vicissitudes of daily living
refine my life
into the Golden Years?
do I deserve this contentment and ease
any more than a homeless refugee deserves
his discontentment and strife?
being proud of my virtuous maneuvers is
apologia pro vita sua
yet my Christian soul tells me that everything
ad majorem Dei gloriam

Originally published in Reflections from the Texas Cradle,
November 2018

THREE HAIKU ABOUT
PRAIRIE CREATURES

flat endless prairie
rare prairie cocks leave tall grass
must be seen to mate

hermitic heron
standing in shallow water
wind blows through salt grass

bubble-throat lizard
between the teeth of my cat
rolls his eyes at me

Originally published in Better than Starbucks, *November 2018*

WHERE I LIVE

nobody has ever heard of where I live
well, my friends have
they call it "East Barnyard"
a name, though sarcastic, I like
yes, I choose to live on this prairie,
it's true
the land is so flat the highways are
infinite
only the tall salt grass
hides the prairie chickens
who need hidden places
during mating season
a coach-whip chased the UPS man
across our yard, one day,
boxes of diapers flying in all directions
he drove off like a rocket launch
copperheads circle my little studio
like Comanche circling the wagons
I come out only when starvation
makes me risk snakebite
Gatsby my cat is afraid of the dogs
who roam the open prairie
maybe they're coyotes,
who knows

 RAY SPITZENBERGER

the bubble-throated lizards are afraid of Gatsby
I'm afraid of Gatsby when he's mad
even the snakes are afraid of Gatsby
everybody needs a prairie cat
there's also beauty where I live
one day the mama armadillo and two babies
came out of her hole under the house
the babies came running toward my wife
who spoke baby talk to them
until the mama came and
nudged them under a bush
nobody has ever heard of where I live
and city folks would hate the snakes
but I know that
like us
they would be overwhelmed
by the beauty
of two baby armadillos

FOUR HAIKU FROM THE PRAIRIE

afternoon hush
invaded suddenly
by rushing squirrel

wheelbarrow
stacked high with bricks
wheel in mud

homesick
Texas prairie life sun-splashed
daughter snowed in

Originally published in Better than Starbucks, *July 2019*

newly hatched tadpoles
circle water poppy
exploring life begins

Originally published in Better than Starbucks, *September 2018*

 RAY SPITZENBERGER

SMALL TOWN CHRISTMAS EVE
IN TWO TANKAS

small town Christmas Eve
asleep in the hill country
Christmas lights still on
at café closed for the night
not a creature is stirring

not even a mouse
caroling long since ended,
its joyful echo
still in hearts of those who heard
and in hearts of those who sang

Happy Christmas to all, and to all a good night!

OPEN SPACES

sitting on the grass
leaning against the trunk
of a native pecan tree
I feel and see
the warm winds
move low hanging branches
with gusts at times
that make mid-summer leaves
look like old hens
with ruffled feathers
the shade and the wind gusts
offering some respite
from the savage Gulf Coast sun
I don't want to leave
the shade and the gusts
and return to work
in the open spaces
to be bathed in the full rays
of that sizzling sun
like most choices in life
consequences determine decisions

so what we do
is often not what we want
necessity dictates reality
and the rapid pace of life
does not allow much time
for a protected space

MY HOMESTEAD, FOR BETTER OR WORSE

for better or worse
I love my homestead
rows of burnt-gold milo maize
the grain sorghum grown for feed
hot sand between long rows
reflects the fierce sun above
and burns bare feet
week after week
wonderfully challenging prairie life
of milo maize fields and hay meadows
plow, plant, plod and slog
reap the sorghum, bale the hay
work hard, week after week
ah, but the clear country sky emboldens
the fresh country air enlivens
the prairie winds invigorate
what freedom to ride your horse
across the endlessly flat land
no subway trains to catch
no tall buildings to block afternoon breezes
no screech-clang-honk-bang of traffic

no long waits in long lines

at the close of the work day

I love my homestead

for better or worse

open and free

Originally published in Empty Silos, *December 26, 2018*

BAD WEATHER IN THREE HAIKU

yard
empty of birds
tornado

clouds
pregnant with hail
child's laughter

river floods
large fingers of water
explore living room

WARMTH STARTS WITHIN: A TANKA

cracks between floor boards
cold wind-fingers slither in
logs in steel belly
rancher's near-frozen face thaws
warmth starts within, moves outward

Originally published in Tanka Journal, *issue #7*

THEY'RE CALLED 'BLACK BEAUTY'

My yard is a retreat center
For the feathered ones,
Who sometimes sing but always have a lot
     to say.
Like today, a party of grackles landed
On my pecan tree, stripped bare
     by winter.
They come every January,
Or at least I think it's the same flock.
Some people can't tell grackles
From ravens and crows,
But that's just humans
     who believe
If you've seen one black bird
You've seen them all.
Most birds are talkers,
And if you listen carefully
     to them,
You'll never mistake one for the other.
Crows "caw" in pleasant repetition,
Ravens "croak" in iterating verbal assaults,
And grackles "cackle" in loud, metallic
     creaking shrieks.

 RAY SPITZENBERGER

How could you really mistake one for the other?!
The same humans, if they're interested at all,
Are only attentive to the "Beautiful Ones," the birds
Who flit and flutter about in their red and blue and yellow
frocks.
Yet, the crow is modishly feathered in denim black,
The raven, in rich, silk ebon, and the grackle,
O the grackle, sports a natty iridescent blue scarf on
          black polyester.
Yes, sometimes grackles do seem a little rude to me,
But never, never to a fellow grack!
Those selective human observers just mentioned
Live in mindless oblivion among
          their own.
Suddenly, one of their own roars by on a side street.
In seconds, the yard is empty, silent,
          and birdless.
Ah, yes, a tree full of grackles,
A raven on the window lattice,
And a yard full of crows!
Such creatures as these attentive ones call
          "black beauty"!

HOUSTON AND ITS PRAIRIE TOWNS STOOD IN WATER

when a lazy river has become a roaring torrent
when a circle of rising water
                surrounds our town
and its sibling rivulets join the siege
water cascades across
highways and county roads
on the other side of our town
the endless rain sends runnels
rushing across the bridges
the old timers have never seen anything like it before
where you can't get in
and you can't get out
here on the gulf plains
a short distance from Houston
which was not even the door
through which Harvey
entered as a hurricane
Houston's flood was
                our flood
long after Rockport and Corpus dried out
long after news coverage ended
Houston and its prairie towns
stood in water

     RAY SPITZENBERGER

LIGHTS

out on the prairie where I live
stadium lights on Friday nights
light up the whole town
for those few hours of bumps and thumps and
   tackles
the rest of the week it's dark
but the prairie grasses shine in the
   moon glow
I have always been able to see so clearly
   in prairie darkness
it's like cataracts are removed from my eyes
things are different in the large cities
so impossible for me to go back to
the lights of cities are ever on
brighter than stadium lights
large cities never sleep
bodies endlessly quick-stepping in
   that light
like the light on a body undergoing surgery
on the prairie
I sleep
I wake
I live

THREE HAIKU IN OCTOBER 2019

October sun
cold light touches
cat's toes

canna leaves
swaying with wind
sun and shadow

sun porch
large windows aflame
lightning flashes

THREE HAIKU OF WINTER

like an iced cookie
stepping stone in wintry rain
cold sleet in Texas

waves slashing the shore
iced waves splashing the highway
cars sliding sideways

snow falling mildly
snow falling near the Gulf
soon it will melt here

THE PUMPKINS SEEM TO SMILE

Autumn has golded up the pumpkin patch
And the pumpkins growing there, though they have no
faces,
. . . yet,
Seem to smile.
The new autumn chill in the air
Sends shivers down the spines
Of the children on a Halloween hayride,
Some already dressed in their Halloween spookiest.
A couple crows fly near to assess the scene.
Suddenly, they lift, tilt and bank away,
Like flying saucers.
The pumpkins seem to smile.

VIEW FROM THE PATIO ROOM

morning coffee
in the patio room
where the walls are windows
to the outside
offering a splendid view
of a backyard
in the prairie town
where I live
leaves sail to the ground
like Sulfur butterflies
the huge clusters of yellow pompoms
disappearing fast
from the trees
the late November sunlight
causes black strips of shadow
to decorate the patio
like a fallen striped awning
in the tall grass
laced with fallen leaves
bristling up here and there
are the bushy tails
of hungry squirrels
searching for food
beauty absorbed
and coffee finished
I can begin my day

HOARFROST

the old man
standing on the porch
surveys his universe
and sees
under the trees
piles of leaves
lying on the floor
of the oak grove
like heaps of hair
around a barber's chair
the trees are bald
not a bird lingers
on cold hands and fingers
only a squirrel persists
in sitting on a frozen arm
as a frosty mist
envelopes the old man's farm
and soon his vision
is blurred by nature's decision
to cover the countryside
in hoarfrost

the trees shudder
in the icy wind
the squirrel scampers in
the hollow of the tree's belly
to a warm nest
the old man shuffles back in
to the warm hollow
of his universe

Originally published in Bitterzoet, *2018*

SUMMER HAIKU

SUMMER 2017

yellow butterfly
mellower yellow sunlight
magic of summer

dove beak sips next to
pale water poppies
afloat in huge black kettle

hanging basket sways
weeds grow with periwinkles
intruders won't leave

SUMMER 2018

lightning bugs sprinkling
tiny lights into dark night
young boy pursues them

loud-voiced little wren
repeats call to empty trees
lawn mower ends call

 RAY SPITZENBERGER

SUMMER 2019

summer heat
dust blows top soil away
ducks on pond

old man
old cat
in front of old fan

late night
cows moan in moonlight
farm deserted

Chuckles

ALTHOUGH MOST LIGHT-HEARTED POETRY IS FOUND IN children's books, adults enjoy funny, even silly, light-hearted verse, too. Perhaps the reason we adults react positively to poetry is the collection of nursery rhymes in our memory bank that we learned in childhood—"Humpty Dumpty," "Jack and Jill," "Pat-a-Cake-Pat-a-Cake," "Hey, Diddle, Diddle," etc. As we got older, we enjoyed limericks, five-line humorous verses, rhyming AABBA, and often written in anapestic trimeter. Usually rude and sarcastic, these may have been the inspiration in the fourth grade for our writing silly little verses in each other's autograph books.

Many funny poems have been written by famous poets over the years, like "A Word to Husbands" and "The People Upstairs," both by Ogden Nash. In the comedies of William Shakespeare, you will find what we would have to consider humor in poetry form. Not-so-famous poets have written funny poems for adults, too.

The first poem I ever published was a humorous poem, "Little Johnny Allfeet" (which was published in my high school newspaper). It was funny, it was about football, and my classmates loved it. Since it marks the beginning of my career in writing and publishing poems, I've included it here.

Light-hearted verse can cause the reader to laugh or smile. Maybe a few of these will bring at least a chuckle.

LITTLE JOHNNY ALLFEET

Little Johnny Allfeet,
In a game did compete.
Coach was so short on men,
He put our little Johnny in.
Pads made his stoop shoulders look wide,
But his skinny legs he could not hide.
From the library he sadly departed,
When that fateful football game finally started.
They told him to block and block did he,
But by mistake, 'twas the referee.
When they sent him out to catch a pass,
He fell and slipped down on the grass,
And he slid
Down the grid
On his head with his legs in the air.
He caught the ball with his feet, but the touchdown was
    fair.
That's why he was called by the football fans,
Little Johnny Allfeet and not any hands

Originally published in The Traveler, *Giddings High School Newspaper, 1949*

RODEO 1940

Out of the chute
Comes the female rider
In quick pursuit
Of the steer beside her.
Its neck she ropes
With highest hopes
Not only that she compete
But the male riders beat!
Her lasso looped the bovine,
Her timing clocked out so fine,
She easily won the round,
Male riders their match they found.

AN OLD CAT

an old cat
a shedding cat
a much loved cat
in spite of that.
my studio, her habitat
there, she sat
in the loft
on the first slat
of a ladder
and leaped to the floor
when she saw me at the door,
a loyal, loving cat
ever eager to see me.
after years in my keep,
she can no longer leap
nor climb the ladder.
an old cat
a shedding cat
a much loved cat
in spite of that.

being unable to climb or leap,
she bunks at my feet
under the drawing table
as I sit down to draw
with reed pen and Japanese ink,
she raises her paw
as if to help me think
an old cat
a shedding cat
a much loved cat
in spite of that

TWO LIGHT-HEARTED HAIKU

old man goes out
old cat comes in
man in, cat out

cat paws door
cat meows . . . cat yowls
old man reads

HAPPY WITHOUT KNOWING IT?

my friends think things
such as new cars and stylish clothes
will bring them happiness
but three wardrobes
and three new cars later
happiness will still elude them
Minirth and Meier say happiness
is a choice
Abe Lincoln said the same thing
and so did W. R. Inge
Vauvenargues once said
there are men who are happy
without knowing it
wouldn't that be awful?
to find out at the end of your life
that you had been happy
all your life
and didn't know it?

DESTINED TO BE EATEN OR HATCHED

it is my habit
to boil a dozen eggs
at a time
but once I used a different pot
and only eleven would fit
one lonely egg
was left behind
in its carton
funny how chance
or circumstance
saved the egg
from dying in boiling water
yet it's only a matter of time, —
it's her destiny to be eaten
or hatched

REFILL THE RELIQUARY WITH JELLIE BELLIES

very old men like me
forget to take their vitamins
as well as their prescribed pills
and we often chew
the bitter ones
even when the label says,
swallow, don't chew
life is short
and very old men like me
are on the short end of short
so we might as well spill out
all our pills
and refill the reliquary
with jelly bellies

A WRITER'S LAMENT

"one can always use
an extra hundred thou,"
the chic say
"make do or do without,"
writers say
"sack groceries,"
I say
Whitman was always
    short of cash
Frost milked cows
    to pay the bills
Dickens sold a chapter
    for a penny
my column earns
    twenty
fame
is no
gain
kudos
buys no
food
no money
no fame
"sack groceries"

EACH DAY WAS THE SAME . . . UNTIL

each day

was the same

was the same

was the same

was the same

was the same

was the same

was the same

was the same

was the same

was the same

until

one day

you came

and brought

fun and laughter

into my life

Written when I first met my wife

FOUR HAIKU:
OLD CAT, STRAY KITTEN

old cat
naps day after day
after day

stray kitten
the "Energizer Bunny"
goads old cat

old cat
fed up with in-your-face
stray kitten

stray kitten
the "Road-Runner"
retreats

AN OLD CAT'S LAMENT

My peeps took in a stray cat
Who is a wild little brat, —
She, a Tasmanian acrobat,
Me, a geriatric, slow and fat.
Yes, I'm an old cat,
Too old for all that!
If my home is to be her habitat,
This then is my demand, my caveat:
Divide the habitat,
Or tell that cat to scat!

THE SMILE

There are many kinds of smiles.
There's the "I-got-a-new-car" smile,
And the "Whoohoo-it's-Friday" smile.
The good joke smile,
The bad joke smile,
The really big smile when you get a raise,
And the disappointed smile when you don't.
But no smile is as big,
As radiant,
As a granddaughter's smile!
So, Lauren,
Or, Avery,
Make a smiley face, —
Just for Grandpa!

THE FLAP-FLAP OF LOST SOLES

at the end of the legs
of old men
are crippled feet
this is my story
this is my bleat
I found what I thought
I needed to wear
a pair of tai chi slippers
such squashy softness
such squishy comfort
perfect for sitting or standing
but soles that slide
are not safe for walking
gluing on a pair of soles
with grips
my cane and I went forth
sprightly and smart
until I heard the flap-flap
of lost soles

TEXAS WENDISH DACTYLIC DANCE

Go to the barn dance at evening glow,
Play the ole fiddle, O, fiddle, O,
Dance to the fiddle and mandolin,
Mandolin, Madelyn, mandolin,
Jan and his banjo, ka-plink, ka, ka –
Plink, ka, ka-plink, ka, ka-plink, plink, plink.
Selma sings, Madelyn dances, with
Mandolin strumming, still strumming, ja,
Evening glowing, music flowing,
Wends dancing and dancing through the night!

THE WREN AND THE HEN

In a muddy pen,
a wren
jumped on a hen,
and the hen
began to spin
and spin,
until the wren
fell off the hen
who left the pen
to chase the wren
who again
jumped on the hen
who again
began to spin
until the wren
flew up with a grin,
and said, "I win!"

ODE TO THEE, LI'L OUTHOUSE

A woeful ode to thee,

O weathered li'l privy.

O where, o where, have you fled,

Family meditation shed?

Thou canst never return,

For I fear thou didst burn.

We shall shed a tear for thee, O faithful privy,

For thou art a part, like we, of family history!

Originally published in Images, The East Bernard Tribune,
*March 3, 1993 (Written shortly after the disappearance of
Mama's old outhouse)*

BOOKS (WITH AN APOLOGY TO JOYCE KILMER)

I think that I shall never e'er look
At a tree as lovely as a book.

A book that feeds each hungry mind
Morsels which ravenous eyes find;

Held up to God for Him to see
Joy flowing from a worm* like me;
*bookworm

A worn book whose pages display
Quick notes scribbled any which way;

On whose cover coffee has rained,
And on whose pages it has stained.

Trees are planted by worms* like me,
*bookworms
Only God can cause poetry.

Acknowledgments

It is only with the professional help of my daughter, Rae Ann Spitzenberger, a book designer in New York, that I am able to publish a second book, *Open Prairies*, after the success of my first work, *It Must Be the Noodles*. Not only was her help necessary, but it has been a joy to work with her. I offer a special thanks to my granddaughter, Lauren Stolle, for the excellent photographs she took for the book. It's not often that a writer has the special, uplifting opportunity to work with two close family members in preparing a book. And, I must thank my entire family for their fervent support of my writing efforts and for being the inspired subjects of a number of my poems. Finally, I must thank my wife, Peggy Spitzenberger, for loving this eccentric old poet unconditionally, and for her abiding faith in my ability as a writer.